Praise for *Addiction Apocalypse*

What is the line between myth and extinction? [...] What is the line between ownership and grace? In Remi Recchia's *Addiction Apocalypse*, poems dance along these lines with lyric intensity and narrative grace. Funny and tender, proud and self-deprecating, this collection chronicles a life of transition, conviction, and addiction, one where *every injection* is *a baptism,* one that dwells in the everyday of Taco Bell, Mike Flanagan shows, rent debt, and 90-day chips, but also reaches for something more, *shout(s) hallelujahs until my throat is sore.* Recchia gives answer to the question, "What happens when the apocalypse is churning in your own body?" The answer is that you survive.

—**DONNA VORREYER,** AUTHOR OF *TO EVERYTHING THERE IS*

"We didn't have the words," says Remi, the trans speaker of "Dead Name," the opening poem in *Addiction Apocalypse.* The word *transition* began as a noun of action, and this is a poetry in the act of finding the much-needed words to talk about the body, to talk about change and hardship, intimacy ("we are always talking") and fulfillment. The *Remi* who speaks in these poems, having, as he says, "waited the dark," articulates beautifully, with an often astonishing honesty, the arduous passage from waiting to action to realization.

—**NANCY EIMERS,** AUTHOR OF *HUMAN FIGURES*

In Remi Recchia's *Addiction Apocalypse*, "transformation" is the vital force underpinning the speaker's core humanity: transformed bodies, transformed minds, transformed relationships, and transformed worlds characterize the lived experience and rich sociocultural landscapes that populate these poems. Simultaneously urgent and playful, Recchia's resonant lyricism stewards the reader on a journey through the complex layers of interrelated change: gender transition and familial loss, renewed spirituality and addiction crisis, mental illness and the whirlwind of new love intertwine. The speaker could try to pull them apart, to hold them separate from one another inside himself, but why would he? A triumph in transmasculine poetics, *Addiction Apocalypse* celebrates the messy, brilliant tapestry of a life lived in refusal of stagnation.

—**JACOB GRIFFIN HALL,** AUTHOR OF *BURIAL MACHINE*

Addiction Apocalypse

Addiction Apocalypse

Poems

Remi Recchia

21st Century Poets, No. 46

TRP: The University Press of SHSU
Huntsville, Texas 77341

Library of Congress Cataloging-in-Publication Data

Names: Recchia, Remi, author.
Title: Addiction apocalypse : poems / Remi Recchia.
Description: First edition. | Huntsville, Texas : TRP: The University Press of SHSU, [2026]
Identifiers: LCCN 2024027009 (print) | LCCN 2024027010 (ebook) | ISBN 9781680034165 (paperback) | ISBN 9781680034172 (ebook)
Subjects: LCSH: Substance abuse--Psychological aspects--Poetry. | Gender identity--Social aspects--Poetry. | Gender identity--Psychological aspects--Poetry. | Belief and doubt--Poetry. | LCGFT: Poetry.
Classification: LCC PS3618.E38 A66 2026 (print) | LCC PS3618.E38 (ebook) | DDC 811/.6--dc23/eng/20240624
LC record available at https://lccn.loc.gov/2024027009
LC ebook record available at https://lccn.loc.gov/2024027010

FIRST EDITION

Cover art by Zeynep Ozdelice | iStockPhoto
Author photo by Jason Wallace, Oklahoma State University, College of Arts and Sciences
Cover design by Cody Gates, Happenstance Type-O-Rama
Interior design by Maureen Forys, Happenstance Type-O-Rama

Printed and bound in the United States of America
First Edition Copyright: 2026

TRP: The University Press of SHSU
Huntsville, Texas 77341
texasreviewpress.org

For my life,
Roseanna,
and our joy,
Emily-Grace

Contents

To love another person
is to see the face of God.

—VICTOR HUGO

I feel furthest from sobriety when I think
of it as purely an absence. Sobriety is a
grace and grace is everything but absent.

—KAVEH AKBAR

I
FIND YOUR SAFEHOUSE

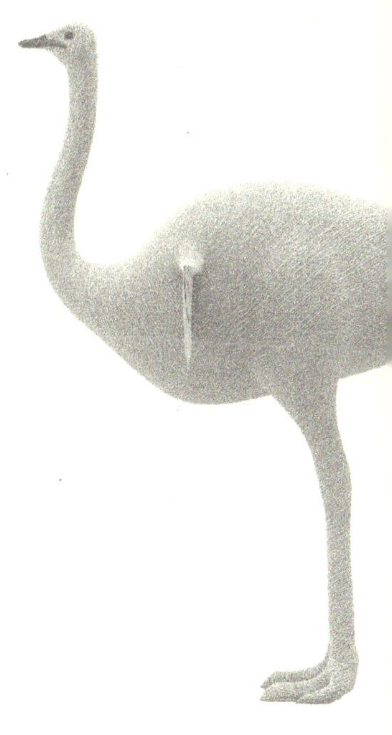

DEAD NAME

For Frank Dubois and other "female husbands," 1883

I still turn when I hear my dead
name at the coffee shop, feel etymological
bomb spray shrapnel across the room.

A blond creature snakes her way to the front
counter, takes steamed milk & chocolate, hands
small like mine, but pretty. My knuckles have

calloused themselves since an early birth
in the early morning. Stained with bar-dust
& forever-bruises. Tar under fingernails.

My new name I bear proudly like an iguana
his jeweled robe, having shed an expired
skin. Every man will ask his wife to keep

a secret. It's up to her whether or not she'll loose
it like a rabid dog. Tabloids come at all
hours. Did Frank Dubois ever stand a chance?

His vagina sealed shut like a secret, his Gertrude
unsmiling. 100 years later & still we believe her
when she says she didn't know.

How long does it take to suffocate
instinct? To bury billions of genes in the making,
passing name down from mother to daughter,

granddaughter from grandmother? We can barely
trace these origins but know them when we see
them. Maybe Frank's husband wouldn't have ripped

his small-town Wisconsin from Frank had he grown
hair & penis like me. Maybe no one
would have noticed. Frank, I will not print your dead

name, won't, though tempted, call your wife
coward. We didn't have the words in the Trans-
continental era, but still we hopped night

trains, swung from circus rafters, seduced near-
death experiences seconds from the tracks. Left
notes folded neatly on goose feather pillows. As a child,

I thought crime around each corner, an inevitability
from the movies I wasn't allowed to watch. I looked
for axes out of my eye corners upon leaning my head

under the faucet for 3 a.m. tap-water gasp, convinced
the sink was a tree stump & the witch in the woods
would execute me at the neck, her blade buried in my last

wishes. But the only witch now is the hunt I'm dodging
with Frank Dubois. He's not behind or ahead, he's with me,
in me, evading this hunt without beagles or guns, French

horn transformed into the echoes of our old names, excess
syllables filling our heads while we strut on the streets
crowded with the girls & deaths we used to look like.

SAILOR'S KNOT

As useless as a car wash in a rain-
storm, my body stands in the shower

without its brain. What I mean to say is my head
hurts. What I mean to say is some days

I throw up heartache. Orange flecks, curled
caterpillar bodies, flop against the toilet seat.

I was too slow to reach the porcelain.
I was too slow to raise my hand, declare myself

present. Who am I, if not the ghoul
you pretend not to hear through your satin pillowcase?

I have always been last, and not, I suspect,
as the Lord intended.

My name, impossible to pronounce, rhymes
with "last call." It is possible to be blind

in love and to be hungover at your own wedding.
If St. Peter cards us at the door, you're screwed for loving me.

The late-heat fireflies bob outside the window
like drunken ships. Or maybe they're the light-

house, hazy, calling the last meal to shore. O,
sailor! o, siren! tie me or take me! Crush my skull

against thunderclouds and sink me with expired
treasure. Indenture me. Give me your timber

and I'll craft the most perfect plank
these glittering Atlantic starfish have ever seen.

BAPTISM | BEFORE I GREW UP, THERE WAS A WAR

Before I grew up, there was a war. Call it predestination, call it manifest destiny, call it nature vs. nurture. The truth of the matter: I was born in the small of the morning without my penis. Before I grew up, there was a war. My soldiers fought & lost, tiny testosterone helmets caved in like melted trumpets & inside-out roses. Genitals flowered & prepared exquisitely the feast.

Now I'm grown & have no need for anaphora urgency. I'm grown—still I lie—& grow larger still in the forest, collecting mushroom caps to wear at masculine revelries. I cover my head in church. I anoint myself with oil even when the priest is not away. Every injection a baptism. I baptize myself over & over again, new needle & prayer each week. My legs are thick like the father's, wrists sore like the son's.

GRAVEDIGGER

The morning finds me cutting celery stalks in the dark hours after I have fled
the bandwagon. Last night's dinner prepared long after scheduled digestion: an
alcoholic's goodnight

kiss. My hands unearth the tiny earthquakes under liver spots & wedding ring. Palms slipping
over green plant belly & root. Stalk standing firmer than my own spine, which is curled like a beast

in hibernation. My shoes lost somewhere on Main Street or Kennedy Ave or the subway
station. My shoes lost because. My feet lost because. My landline lost because marriage means

I must carry a line to shore. The celery screams & I cannot, my tongue bruised whale
gray & algae purple from everything nobody wanted to notice. The only constant in life is that a bar-

tender will only cut you off once he finds, upon pillaging your pockets, that you are empty.
When I was young, my shadow spoke to me. It said, *Remi, why don't you ever look where you're going?*

GIFTS

God gave me arthritis, twisted joints & inflamed nerve / God gave me a wife / God gave me a student loan / I said this debt is insurmountable / God gave me a pet dog / God gave my dog arthritis, twisted joints & inflamed nerve / God gave me a home / I said I can't afford the mortgage / God gave me a flood / God gave me a teapot / I burnt my hand on boiling water / God gave me shimmering cysts / God scraped the earwax from my throbbing canals / My power went out / God gave me tired / God gave me directions / I lost the map like a pirate his treasure / God gave me a light / I smoked it all up / God gave me a body / I said wait it doesn't fit quite right / God gave my wife arthritis, twisted joints & inflamed nerve / God gave me a job / I showed up late & got fired / God gave me white spots on the brain / God gave me an MRI / God gave me a CAT scan / God picked out my maple wood coffin / God said I'm sorry my gifts are not enough

PAYING FOR TOP SURGERY IS LIKE GOING TO DEBTOR'S PRISON

in that you'll never be able to pay it off,
not really. You could apply for a loan and count
temporary zeros in your bank account, dwindling
to nothing while your interest puts on muscle. The debt,
you'll tell your mother, is worth the debt of your body.
Maybe if you get drunk enough on the weekends
or weekdays or weak evenings you'll start to fantasize
bread knife and Ibuprofen, a homegrown operating
room sterilized enough to siphon off excess tissue.
You might sneak into the exclusive Safari Zoo
exhibit and aim your binoculars everywhere but the camels'
pale, malnourished humps, then start a GoFundMe
and Photoshop a flat camel with the caption,
Liberate All Mammals Now. You might buy an ugly
tarp at Home Depot and drape
it over the bathroom mirror to shield
your eyes from that perverse double-moon.
Maybe you sign up for a monthly gym membership
with what little money you have and work off
the fat. Maybe take diet pills. Is denial a placebo?
You could commit insurance fraud. The arsonists
do it all the time. You could look that sales rep
right in her marble blue eyes, say, *yes, I'm a breast-
cancer risk, I need the doctor to defuse these ticking
time bombs. This ticking in my brain.* You know
it's not really a lie. Maybe you'll rob a bank or two,
run away into fabled glory, getaway car ready to cut
through the thick western night. You'll smoke
with your friends around the campfire as you count
murders of cash, flocks of dimes, schools of copper.
You'll make up secret birdcalls and warning signs.
You could call your wealthy friends and make up an extravagant
lie. A wedding, perhaps, or funds to build a new end-
days bunker. A down-payment on a house.
You'll have to avoid the word "elective."
Or you could cut down on groceries by half,

then three-quarters, then entirely. An extra [   ] per month will almost cover the operating room in about two years. You'll watch your skeleton sharpen and eyes glaze over as you deprive, deprive, deprive. Throw in the trowel, Remi. Dig deep. The prison invitation says, *BYOM: Bring Your Own Manacles. Black tie optional.*

SINKER

Small & on the floor, I am pressed
under another boy's knees. He offers
my lips a dustpan of flies. The flies are dead:
miniature gray soldiers with wings
for bayonets. My mouth remains
shut. The boy's friend is in the background,
guarding the door to the gymnasium.
I squeeze my eyes so tight I see
white stars & galaxies & pinwheels
charting refusal. Footsteps sound
like a cannon in the hall. A teacher or
Cerberus. The boy drops the dustpan
& I bury myself in flies.

FIRST

What would you say now,
my first, knowing that I'm bigger?

That my forearms' muscles have muscles?
That while I used to trim sparingly,

I now cut nothing except the golden follicles
crowning my head like an ostrich his plumes, blooming

deep black and handsome
cream. Soon I will resemble my whiskered

father. I try his ties on in the mirror and always
resist the hook. My eyes have laid

perfect eggs in praise
of the future. They tremble

under the noonday sun. Phantom pain
echoes through my ring finger. It remembers the promises

we branded to our skin when we were sick
and young in love. You worshipped a girl

who did not exist. My right thigh, once
lined with hazards, is a safely zoned construction

site. Up close, a man can see the dots marking
intramuscular self. A transformation

as glorious as the cross. Who can wear
me on his neck. Who can stomach the dawn.

GHAZAL FOR THE BUMPS ON MY SPINE

They appeared overnight, two knobs flowered
on bone and tendon. Lumps kissing like the petals of a flower.

The doctor's cool hands traced across my back
like a box turtle swimming through algae and flower.

Medical bills, houses we've left, your mother
calling home. I always bring her flowers.

I imagine the bumps as miniature, under-the-skin
cacti. They sleep in my sand, waiting to flower.

Instead of sheep, I count the bumps in the dark.
They swell against white bedsheets, prickling like flowers.

My bones don't know *emergency.* They know *slow, chronic*
prescription bottle breath. They know *lingering deep like the roots of a flower.*

I undress in the light before you. Flat chest and slight belly.
Will you forgive my ineptitudes? I buy you rings and flowers.

Do the bumps on my spine match the white spots lighting
up my brain? Has my life, all along, been a rotting flower?

The bumps grow and grow. They play make-believe:
when I'm older, one says, I'm going to marry a flower.

Oh, Remi, you've missed them, those sly warning signs.
To do on Monday: browse caskets, sing church hymns, burn flowers.

DEAR HIRING COMMITTEE:

I want to say I'm qualified for this job, that I have been the hardest
worker, the kindest colleague, the most promising student. I want to say
hire me—you won't regret it!

The attached resumé, however, may indicate that instead of saying
sorry, I just say, pass the salt, that I tend to bury others' wounds in the sand
under me like the ostrich I am, stuffed in human clothes.

I bring baked goods to work potlucks: soft, expired Wal-Mart cookies
intended for the dentist as much as for the boss. My friends make
ravioli from scratch, shrimp linguini, chocolate torte, and I have no qualms

devouring them. I spill coffee over keyboards, hang up the phone before
pressing transfer, concede to my hangover with my face slumped
over the warm, humming computer monitor.

Sure, I can get the job done: I always found the ghost in the graveyard before my
friends, our faces sticky with the sweat unique to children. I always knew
when to push too far, when to say the right wrong thing to be taken out

and taken home. My references will, I'm sure, reference me, though how
well, I could not say. Do employers keep track of late punch-cards, missed
meetings, typo-ridden company memos?

Take me out to lunch. Let me show you how well I can behave with some-
thing between my teeth. I'll let you shove my hand aside when I pretend to reach
for the check. I'm missing first, last, and deposit. I can start right now.

ARE YOU OKAY, MIKE FLANAGAN?

An open letter to the creator of The Haunting of Bly Manor, The Haunting of Hill House, *&* Midnight Mass

I've noticed that your characters can't stop
drinking. I see hazy shots of self-
control crashing into gutters, windows, vampire

tombs in Israel. I see ghost-spire & castle-
knot. I see a grief so far gone it would rather haunt the screen
than stay folded in your wallet. Dani could save everyone
except herself. Theodora padded her body in black
leather. The priest, though faithful, raised

hands to the wrong god. Are you okay, Mike Flanagan?

I see jewels & smoke, hint of jukebox
burrowed in dusty crawl space. I see the wrong
earring on the wrong ear. I see
an affair in the window. Are you okay, Mike Flanagan?

I see myself in your rivered plots. I see my puke
caressing the needle like a song.
I see my elbows, throat, fingers, wrists
bruised by a hobgoblin twice my size. I see

rehab door & attic confiscating anything sharp
or ingestible. I see my DUI mirrored in Riley Flynn's
blue-red ribboned dreams. Am I okay, Mike Flanagan?

Mike, I see the gray matter of your brain, slipping
into the same plot on loop. Mike, I recognize
the impulse to graffiti your trauma on everyone's bed-
room walls, to present your shortcomings like a to-do

list. Our prayers are not unusual, Mike, shriveled dry
lips the only things sober in the confessional.

I see shotguns shaped like angel's wings, I see
bread that is actually poison, I see rowboats
divorced from nursery rhyme, I see dance studio
behind red door, I see tree house warped
in Steven's mind, I see sunspots on your brain.

I see you, Mike Flanagan. Mike Flanagan, I see you.
I see you & I know that in the end, when you no longer
know yourself, you're lighting that candle for me.

LINKED HAIKU WITH EX-BOYFRIEND & TREE SAP

My face is naked
Shards of mirror in the sink
Fish drown sometimes, too

*

Your mind is stunning
I love the way you showed me
trees have answers, too

*

Phone calls in my head
Late nights, pointless loving
numb my brain like ice

If a Quaker shoots himself,
is it ironic or is it just sad?

*

Sometimes I get high
I call my mom, don't speak
static 'round the wire

*

Wait for me to loose
this noose around the bough
sticky with dried sap

*

Doctor, please prescribe
me a joke—am I the joke?
Are thorns blooming, too?

*

My darling, come home
I won't eat without your hands
sweeping ants out, too

If a Quaker loots himself,
is he thief, or is he thieved?

*

I flush all my pills
They can join the fish, grow
toxic dorsal fins

*

Come return my heart
My chest crumples from the gap
Stoned like the wolf, too

Is a Quaker's promise moot
if he won't swear an oath?

*

Books are just dead trees
giving & giving freely
We steal sap & run

*

Doctor, how to best
burn a lover's leftovers?
Toothbrush, jacket, toad?

*

My god demands peace
Yours is maybe violent
Revenge sown so deep

*

I've thrown your boots out
Stars delete your voicemails
Razors buried whole

YOUR THERAPIST HAS SURFER DUDE ENERGY

and maybe you want to fuck him but he's charging you
$120 an hour, and you are not a John. Save what's [not]
in your pants for Friday night.

You are allowed to sit on his couch
only when riding the right wave of crazy. Depression?
Boring. Anxiety? Trite. Give him a personality
disorder so abstract he'll want to hang it in the Louvre.

He smiles expectantly at your griefs, jots
down, patient regressing as predicted. Not tubular,
dude. Your therapist wipes gold bangs
from his forehead, his brow waxy like a surfboard.
His world clicks together, your grief closing the ape-hominid
divergence, when you admit to

restriction   expulsion   getting high before sex   carrying condoms even
though you will never need them on your trans boy cock   drunk driving every
Tuesday

Your therapist wants you to get pulled over so he can get a good
whiff of the arrest record, the officer's masturbatory
caress of crime on paper. You'll put on the appropriate, pained
face hollowed with shame and bitterness. Your mother's disappointment.

Does he have problems, your therapist?
Is he married? Is he sober? Does he wash his speedo after each
use, as directed? Sometimes you fantasize

his arms at night in the bathroom when the cicadae
are the only witness to your broken. Your small

leg space wrapped between his emergence, his California
tan so real it's fake burning against your skin—oh, the things
you dream about in session! But you're crazy and he is
probably a sadist, and the natural order of things dictates
you leave his dick alone.

In the car after he's drained you
of your weekly terrors, you sit quietly in the tremoring
light. The sun against your cheek like a bomb.

TABERNACLE

My mother taught me to eat clam in 2001,
short lesson of desire and restraint
at the French seaside. *Voici*, she said, guiding
small hands with a scorpion's precision, *break it open*
like a surprise you're not allowed to tell.

The white secret creamy against my tongue,
my jaw the clam's new tabernacle.
I scraped my crooked front teeth along the crevices of the shell.
Once the silk treasures had settled in our hollows,
my twin and I ran to the water
singing *les moules, les moules, grâce*
à Dieu pour les moules, her skirt spinning
shadows under my soft purple vest.

(When the planes hit that fall, my first question:
what's in a bomb?)

Years later, I would swallow another man's
white offering and tell no one.
This is how it is in war.

Is my body a war? This strange vestige
of uterus and penis? Is my clitoris a dick
just because I say it is? Surely
the question is what we make it.

Or, perhaps: is my church a war? The new priest
rhapsodizing not in fear of the end but in the could-be
glory of today while old whiskered men
sit and stare in dissent. I have seen that stare
before. I have been that stare before
and am, in fact, that stare right now,
across the Atlantic and two decades, and men
have always dissented to me. My skin a snailed

contortion of fact and desire. My voice
the echo crawling in their ears at night.

I strip in the mirror and paint the bath-
tub with my freckles. As I reach for cloth
with which to worship my body
like a Christ, I hear Toulouse
chanting in my blood. *Les moules, les moules,*
grâce à Dieu pour les moules.

FROM ACORN TO OAK, OR, AFTER BUT NOT BECAUSE OF SURVIVING THE UNSURVIVABLE, I BECOME A MAN

where once i rolled tight like a snail but was broken
into, i now stand tall like a firmament. a beastly
jaw had wrapped around my dry coating. it licked the cupule
until, unwillingly, i opened. my pericarp sat very, very
still while my insides were destroyed. intentional as a man
prying apart a buttered lobster. afterward all that remained—
a rattle. my ruination took root in a damp
red soil. i waited & fractured, brown molecules spreading
thin & spreading anything but rumor. i waited
years. i waited the dark. & then, somehow, impossibly, i
sprang, knotted-veined with sap sticking to bark like a compass to mercury
magnet. i ordered refills at the pharmacy for vials of thick
gold oil, signed waiver upon waiver excusing arborists from culpability.
my tenderest parts grew outward. i sprang like a pacifist
soldier, an illiterate professor. that is to say: i sprang without reason.
but my branches shone golden in the haze, a triumph
painted against dawn & dusk leaves. branches, leaves,
home. i erect my own shade. i please
myself in the sun. i've grown where i once was shredded,
harboring my shell under a cool blue light.

REMI WITH GHOST & JOAN OF ARC

"I recognized him," she explained, "because my Voice told me. It said to me, 'There he is.'"

My beard twitches at the row of glassed-in past selves on the mantel-
piece & considers razing down the whole display—each photo slandering secret

boy body with *girl, woman, daughter*. Thin hands & thinner waist, I was a Joan of Arc
without the courage. Just the voices. *Remi, who. Remi, when.*

I have unfathered my father a girl. Daydreamed myself in a yellow
construction hat & bulky tool belt. The jobs I never learned to fail.

Perhaps one day I will (un)father a girl. I will (un)bless my wife with lineage,
though she could easily birth a tiny someone of her own. I've heard adoption

has its traumas, but so, too, does a lifetime of mistakenness. I trace my strong
thigh where once it was accused of thickening, of widening like the fatted Easter

calf. Full of triglycerides. In truth, I've always been a map instead of a globe.
I've never been one to carry a compass. The magnet is in my body.

With every injection, I mythologize old shoes—ballerina flats with sparkles,
size 8—worn-out purses—pleather & leather—paper umbrellas for fashion, not function.

What is the line between myth & extinction?
My family wouldn't know me now. A blue-jean-wearing, church-going, straight

married man has replaced the shy ghost that once quailed under the fire
eyes of God. What is the line between ownership & grace?

Joan didn't flinch under heat wave or sly sword. She carried her visions
like a hawk caresses its prey in steel talons.

I know we're not the same person, that an echo doesn't always return to its maker.
I don't know when I'll return to my maker, but when I do, I know it will be in my final

scorched form: low-voiced & micro-dicked, eyes swallowing flame & calling God's name.
Not with supplication, but with praise. With triumph.

II
HOW WILL WE GO ON LIVING

HOW WILL WE GO ON LIVING

Sometimes the hole is a trick hole.
This is the happiness you have.
If you've ever doubted that a body can transform completely,
there is no special God to refer to.
The big basin of yourself
already mourning the men.

*

We would never have guessed that this would be our last meal here,
sun-chapped and hungry feast in an age of fumes.
You should fly from the burning if you can.
Father I was amazed I could find none
but I could still hear the voices.
You'll admit it was no way to live or even keep alive.

*

Faraway radio voices
give me the courage not to need Judas.
They had much to forget.
They went to sea in a sieve.

*

In my younger years
I knew what slant of light
swirled like a hurricane, quiet as the storm's eye.
I wrote silences, I wrote the night.
All things that find a death,
although clumsy,
their bones whiten in the frequent wave.

*

It was a difficult childhood.
Another private sunrise escapes me.
All the stories I keep to myself tell how violence broke and made me.
My heart is as some famine-murdered land
crouched so low to the ground.

*

Soon sleep will be taken away.
Incredible, incredible gravity you lead me here.
For the rest of my life my eyelids were broken.
The birds are silent in their nest.

*

I see the moon and the moon sees me.
The lights are on. The house is empty. Night comes.
What is the texture of kindness?
How long has it been since you told him you loved him?
The holy have left, we know.
A hero's resting place is only as good as the grass he lays his head on.

*

I was born in the room where my mother ate her first hamburger
off the turnpikes of America.
When the weather cleared, it was lovely.
When the night gapes wider
in the room they will not be delicate.

*

Am I dreaming or conjuring?
As if my lips have learned to weep,
he's here again.
Whose skin was the last to touch his?
To whom does it belong?
You, like all of us, are what you conceal.

*

I need your teeth in me, slow and vicious
and tinfoil wrappers crumpled and shimmering.
I long to taste the world with a kiss.
I could love you until my jaw is but memory.
Your eyes are tiny glass windows glittering:
a creature of a fiery heart.
We earned this paradise.

*

Wherever you are, calling you, urgent come in.
A sword stands up between my hips.
There is a house in me. It is empty. I empty it.
I cut my head off and threw it in the sky.
Our throats were boxes of soot
and the birds I'm talking about are not birds at all.

*

Brilliance is a carcass
to stay in your dimly lit rooms.
Remember beauty, which exists, and truth, which does not. Notice that the idea of truth is just as powerful as the idea of beauty.
I realized shuddering these thoughts were not eternity.
Quiet feels round as a planet
explaining, correctly, that I had turned into her shadow.

*

The giver risks madness.
Hope for everything. Expect nothing.
The bronzed bell of the super moon
away the stars but city lights glitter.
Also snow. And the sky, of course—
the land has been blasted by it.
Open up the graves collapsed around all of your trapped, twitching dead.

Our babies are always our babies.
Every angel is terrifying.
For all I know, God could be.

*

I'm nobody! Who are you?
You're the last person on earth prepared for the death of your parents.
My body is estrangement.
I haunt these chambers but they belong to cruel churchified insects.
I am about to be delivered.
What is a wound but a flower,
observations by the spine.
Relieve this intolerable pain!

*

The sky I'd always lived under bulging with huge, unfamiliar stars
our own Old Testament with all the same beheaded kings.
I didn't start this to break anyone's heart.
I puff out my thin and naked chest and stride outside.
At night your legs, love, are boulevards leading me beggared and hungry.
A fever rattled in your throat.
A miracle! That knocks me out.

*

Fish learn from the water to be fish
until sugar and pressure claim his two eyes.
Bone against bone—
this dirt, I have always had it in my mouth.

*

Love is apart from all things.
A shroud I see and I am the shroud, I wrap a body and lie in the coffin.
How will we go on living.

III
ADDICTION APOCALYPSE

THINGS I CAN'T TELL MY LANDLORD

I.

Ronnie, I'm not saying I'm a liar but sometimes
my rent is late not because my boss spelled my last name
wrong on the check again and the bank had to bounce it back again
but my rent is late because I, Remi, am just a man
who is always having a hard week
and yes, I spent it on dried
pineapple and a new watch.

I know I said I wouldn't get a cat.
Cats can't do the dishes or take out
the trash. They can't even talk
right. But screw it, I got a cat and named him
Green Bean, and I wake to his tongue
gifting away at the hair on my head, bathing
me like we're brothers
so hard I worry he'll van Gogh my ears.

He sits in a wooden chair
like a person.
I sit in a wooden chair
like a person.

I don't know who filed that noise
complaint, but yes, that was me
hollering like a bull in heat last August.
No guests, just me. I guess
you could say we all know our own bodies
best, and anyway, I just had to unwind.

Ronnie, have you ever gotten to the end
of your rope? Watched the fibers
unravel at the ends like a useless, one-eyed snake?
Thought about calling your mother or leaving a note and deciding, instead,
that you'll ask St. Peter

not to run the news in the paper just this once?
Have you ever written a will
for your cat even though he snores
and pretends the gas he passes from his perfect
furry anus is yours?
Have you ever loved another creature
so fully you let him eat your toenails?

Ronnie, I have stared down the end of my rope, I have hanged
my last slippery Remi on a barrel,
I have shot my eyes out
underwater. But underwater—wait.

Underwater there are fishes big and golden and grand
as dinner plates, gold as a school
bus in the rich kids' school district where the jailors—I mean
janitors—almost make a living wage, and underwater
there are lionfish that stand tall like mermen before we took
their staffs and there's enough space for Green
Bean to plant his own vegetable garden where he could grow
rutabagas and turnips and carrots
sharp as the Catskills, sharp as the blister in my eye.

II.

Let me begin again.

My cat eats sleeping pears
for breakfast. I dice them carefully, one
velvet bite per saber fang.
Green Bean dives into his bowl face first, tunnel-
visioned joy and gratitude. Some
might call this greed.

If Green Bean could spell, Ronnie, I'm sure
he'd put a curse on you. His paws
rising in furry power. His eyes their own crystal

balls. Ronnie, sometimes I regret removing his testicles.
My ghost-balls squirm at the thought of an unforevering.

But mine aren't ghosts, are they?
A phantom has to have lived
before the pain.
Sometimes I wonder what God was thinking:
no balls, no sperm, no phallus for Remi?
I can't think of anyone yearning
more for fatherhood. But, anyway,

Ronnie, I'm sure you don't care about my trans-
formed genitals. You're too busy waging war
against the working class. And really, with everything
else going on, these flying circuses, these melting
planets, these wax faces, these winged masks, these falling
monkeys, these hungry mice, these strangled gasoline
pumps, these rotten teeth, these translucent stop
signs, these sour trees, these bitter shovels—this is what you want?
To draw money out of Green Bean and me
like blood from an expired gemstone?

We have NOTHING, Ronnie, and still you take EVERYTHING
until we are anemic. I schedule organ transfusions for my bank
account because your vampirism has become
an addiction, hasn't it?

Ronnie, I know about addiction. I know the pull
of the needle and the gleam of the glass. Nothing
feels better than that fix. I bet you lie

naked at night next to your wife—is she greedy, too?—
atop a bed of money, Benjamin Franklin buttering
your biscuits, inhaling the green cash like the rest of us
count herbivores, rounding up to the next dollar and cent and dime.

What would you do if I knocked on your door?
Said, *hey, man, we're late for the next*
meeting. Said, *if we rush we can get to the sixth*

step. We'd show up, the two of us, lord
and lorded, pouring each other
burnt coffee in paper Dixie cups, eyelids
growing dizzy from secondhand smoke.
I'd hold your smooth hand while we mumbled
Our Fathers and counted strangers'
birthdays. Then we'd go home, I guess,
and I'd still owe you money.

Do I sound bitter, Ronnie? Do I sound
hurt? I don't know if I'm hurt but I know an accordion-
scream when it unfolds, a dramatic harpy
organ. Sometimes I am an accordion-scream.

Green Bean plays me
like a piano. He sinks his paws
into the softness I wish was firm, kneading retracted
claw against stretchmarks and well-
worn hips. He curls his head on my flat
chest and runs his tongue-hooks along the bristles
spilling over my tank top, itching for connection.

AT A BASEBALL GAME IN NINETY-DEGREE WEATHER, THE MAN IN FRONT OF ME

tells his girlfriend that one day he woke up and couldn't stop eating
chicken. Pounds and pounds, he says. His tongue wrapped around
fillets. Warm skin rooted itself in his receding gumline. The local

grocery store ran into a shortage. The store manager fired his supplier,
then himself when he could no longer bear the shame of emptiness.
Eventually, the whole place shut down. But this was before we met,

he assures his girlfriend. I'm not that poultry guy anymore. His sun-
tanned hands rub ghost-fat, now cave, beneath an orange sports jersey.
I pull my own T-shirt over my weight. I'm not a hollow bird anymore.

It's the third inning and still the man talks over his girlfriend. She
betrays nothing—no eyeroll, no newsfeed scroll—but I don't think
for a moment that she has no internal reaction to this, that she believes

the man beside her had once destroyed an entire company's livelihood
with his wanting alone. What do they want when they're alone together?
Does he snore? Does she burrow in enough blankets or wake up

with cold feet that may match those on which she'll teeter years
later in white lace and snaked embroidery? Or maybe they haven't yet
seen each other under the indicting bedside lamp, a generic

gift from the man's late grandfather. You can't resent what you don't
know. My hands know more about cradling a curveball than keeping
someone else safe. The Cowboys steal second base as the sun keeps

watch over the fifth inning. I baptize this couple with sweat,
the chicken man and his skinny future. A metal bat slices the wet
air. Perspiration darkens the back of the man's white cap and now even

the woman has collected a sheen. I keep my eyes on the scoreboard,
wonder if I'll make it home in time for lonely nine o'clock cable
and a table set for one. I wonder what it's like to be in love. That is to say:

I wonder what it's like to be perfect. The pitcher on his proud
mound looks like a giant ant. Commander of the colony. Every
player has legs born to serve the glory of his body. Does he eat

chicken for breakfast, lunch, and dinner? Does he swallow wings and cut
his teeth first on night-bones, then dawn-tendon? He takes in gristle
and spits out perfection, rising over the diamond, the bleachers,

the gods, hovering over the chicken man and uplifting him, he
who was once feathered—the pitcher and witness rising together—
and I watch as their cleats block out the sun like talons.

ON LEARNING OF A FRIEND'S SUICIDE WHILE WAITING IN LINE AT THE LOCAL TACO BELL

I got the call mid-order, my eyes locked on the digitized
Crunchwrap Supreme glowing like a beast on the menu board.
I have some news, your brother said. *You might want to sit
down for this.* The beast could bathe in unlimited queso
on my plate. *It's Tyler*, he said. *He's dead.*

A blurring of space. The quesadillas and fiesta potatoes
suddenly unapproachable. The slushie machine a wasteful
aberration. The sixteen-year-old cashier accusing
me with *Sir? Sir?* as if she could not see I was dying.

My feet melted and stuck to the floor, took root like fried
beans seared to the bottom of a to-go box. And to think
I once was hungry.

This is imagined.
Your gun that you named *father* is not.

That is also imagined, in a way.
What your father did to you is not.

Must we always grow into them? Our fathers? Men
that were once boys thin or fat, mean or sweet, settled into complacency
among ex-wives and ex-lives? Your life I worshipped
for a time. I would rush across town at the slightest

threat, give stop signs a passing glance, treat
one-ways as if they had infinite dimensions. I was there
when you bought your first gun, watched you stroke
the trigger like a pet not yet submissive.
Does that make me complicit?

Maybe. But I think you found death as inevitable as seeing
your face in the mirror: still yours, but incorporeal.
A phantom self spun into the ether.

I am sorry I couldn't save you, but come: I can make
you a plate. I can pile burritos and hot sauce and beef
nachos—everything you could never afford—on top of your appetite
endlessly. I can eat tacos and tortillas until I throw up and expel
my endless grief in the Taco Bell bathroom until
they close the lobby and then I'll hop in a car, drive to the next
town, eat more and more until I burst and turn into your image,
belly up on the bathroom floor tiles, suicide note stuffed inside my mouth
with my brain curled up
next to me like a caterpillar.

TRIPTYCH: TO THE PEOPLE I NEVER HIT DRUNK-DRIVING

I.

I hope you have lived long and well. I hope you never again fear a swerving car, head-
lights off like a box turtle's neck protected inside an unwell shell. Skittering like a joke.

I hope you've survived breakups. Survived cancer. Died of something like old age or
a quiet pneumonia, family gathered in jewels and affluence. Has your only hardship been
overdue

credit or a lost cat or a snow shovel bent nearly in half from bitter, resentful black
ice sleeping under your Michelin tires? Or maybe a lukewarm purgatory at the DMV
for a brand-

new driver license for your prodigy of a son? A too-smart son for drinking. A too-smart son
my mother didn't have, who may turn into a too-smart husband my wife didn't have.
Need I go on.

II.

Do you think of me, sometimes, at the liquor store, when you gaze at expensive wine,
debate
Chardonnay or Merlot for the department soirée? The reds and whites gleaming at
you not

as they did for me—an echoing siren's call—but as a friendly wave, saying pick me,
pick me?
I have always been chosen last. In Mr. Samson's gym class, neither boys nor girls
wanted me.

I can't say I blame them. I always threw too hard or too soft. The ball knew I was afraid,
could feel my tensing too-small hands. I hope you know—though I know you've no way

of knowing this—that I don't drink anymore. That I don't even have a car. That I
surrendered my license willingly. I'm without a picture.

III.

I remember the screams of my ex-wife on I-94 when she was not my ex-wife. On I-95.
I-80.
Same sounds, different roads. The steering wheel fast and lucky. I could taste her heart
palpitations

in my throat, hear her jaw set in my brain, which was already, of course, with the
next sip
preoccupied. A meal of amber. Like Christ's, but dimmer. Maybe some powder. When
the divorce

papers came, I barely opened these hazy blue eyes that I must have tricked God into
gifting
me. My pupils were not born glassy. I knew what those papers must be, and so I
signed them.

I signed my life—I mean my wife—away on every dotted line. I agreed to child support
and alimony and her new husband. I bet she trims his beard now. Mine unravels.

Addendum

I still come in the shower, alone, water steaming and streaming down my thighs.
I still watch the news and vote and get to church on time. I shout those

hallelujahs until my throat is sore, until I feel my ears start screaming. I'm thrown
into memories of my first rock concert at fifteen, my date a neon-pink-haired

girl, my brow glinting with that ridiculous piercing. We took ourselves too seriously.
But that night we got lost and jumped and sacrificed pretention for adoration

of the lights and the beat and the thump of something brighter. I smelled beer
but wasn't tempted. I danced and everyone was watching. I just wanted you to know.

THE MEN AT HOME

The men at home have fishing nets. Newport cancer
dangles from their lips. They rise early & park trucks
first in line at the organic foods store. Eighty years after the storm,
the farmers are rich. In the Dust Bowl, noise is the most accepted

form of masculinity. If you're a man, you have to shout.
Soft voice? Shout with your dick. The men at home marry young.
If he's twenty, he's got a child. If he's seventeen, he's got three.
The men at home keep their sperm count healthy.

My pants hang loose around my waist like a failed
jailor. The seams have nothing to guard. The fly
lies, flattened, like a death in a spider's web. Sometimes
I am a death in a spider's web.

The men at home buy women
dinner & get angry if they don't like it.
The men at home take women
to bed & get angry if they like it.

His orgasm is the most important
offering on Sunday. He'll listen to the bells &
choirs, the sermon preaching words misinterpreted,
misattributed, but mostly to his own desire.

After church, the men at home go to IHOP
with their wives. They place big orders & expect
big food. Something they might have killed
in the first place.

I grow a beard as quickly as I can, cross days
off the calendar while new hormones cloud my pores.
I punch a wall when my prescription is delayed.
I order the essential oils man kit online & tell no one.

My beard grows thick & bushy like a mountain man's
(& that's not the only thing that grows). My shoes fit
the same. Do my eyes change color. Does my smile fit
better. I don't recognize myself in the mirror.

The rough, tired faces never burn as much as I'd expect:
The men at home must wear sunscreen. Do their wives rub
it into them in the early morning? Do they rise together,
make love, & kiss each other's skin with white

chemicals? Protection against the sun is the strongest love.
It's a fool's errand, I know, to try to blend in. But still
I mold my ready fists into yard gloves from Dick's
Sporting Goods & browse lawnmowers at John Deere.

My small hands won't know how to pull the cable,
but the blade will work just fine. & that's the point, isn't it?
To cut something down until it's thin & barren. To leave
like it never existed.

NINETY DAYS

We're standing at the ocean, a used sea-
shell peering nervously through your beehive.
Sunday trash blinks up at us through sandy
exoskeletons and footprints. It will strangle the seagulls
when they touch down to feed. Maybe in the dawn. Maybe in the dark.
Maybe the crabs will have gone home by then, tucked
in their pincers and blue blood.

Is the seagull nocturnal? I can never remember—
some poet!—but I remember the joke well:

What do you get when you cross a bird with a sting ray?

Beloved, this beach would wash your face out
if you were but one freckle less lovely.
When I showed up late to our first
date, I should have dropped to my knees
in the middle of that parking lot, rested
mismatched shoes on bird shit and magicked
my way to an instant one-year sobriety chip.

In this mythos, I am golden clean before
we wed. In actual fact, I am ninety days sober
seven years after the first blackout avalanche, and your eyes
startle me in the shock of the sun.

What do you get when you cross an alcoholic with a train?

At the water's mouth, now, curled lip where the tectonic
motion sneaks toward our feet, I wonder
if you can hear my pulse. I cradle it in my swollen
coronary arteries, feel its echo in my bruised-for-two liver.
I wonder if you'll believe me when I say, yes,
my pupils have always been this large.

THE LIGHTS

Under lights & cover bands we moved, dripping rum & sweat
down buttons, down beards, down flies—I was your toad
prince, your helicopter at Rapunzel's Tower: always crashing
when I could be climbing, falling when I could be standing,
as if glued to the floor like a lime fallen from a Tequila shot-
glass clear as the moon over water pulling my shoelaces
knotted into a sand grave, my feet capering on top of the deep
water trench like a marionette without strings but somehow
still guided from above by a gray-faced man; his fingers crawled
over my inhibitions & said *jump jump little toad I know you*
can hear me & I said *but what if my card gets declined*
again but he didn't care—he saw that statement in the mail,
that thin, unassailable indictment, stretched invisible under
black lights & throbbing tongue-sore, & the gray-faced
man's smile looked an awful lot like the River Styx: slightly
sideways & dividing lies from truth & that's the problem,
isn't it? We could never tell when the lights would drown.

FOOTBALL TAILGATE: FIELD NOTES

Observation #49: We are the only conspicuously gay tent.

*

Observation #21: The tuba player is fat. The color guard is thin. Look closer to see how they are all the same.

*

Observation #56: A tall man wears school spirit overalls. I suspect he is not a farmer and thus has no need for overalls. Then again, I am also not a farmer.

*

Observation #4: I see Matthew Shepard when I look in the mirror. I am not Matthew Shepard but at a different time and in a different place I could be.

*

Observation #12: I have never seen so much booze in one place before, and I was raised in a brewery. I rub my 90-day chip between my thumb and forefinger like a rosary.

*

Observation #40: It may rain soon. I hear the ambulance across town.

*

Observation #33: At the middle-school Youthquake, I was informed to let the Lord wash over me. All I wanted was to stand in the tidal wave of another man.

*

Observation #62: My friend Andrew is frail but exuberant, and, I'm guessing, wearing a rainbow thong. My friend Paul woke up blacked-out. My friend Peter brought the deck of cards. It's an heirloom from his parents.

Yes, I am naming Apostles now.

*

Observation #15: Thunder merges with a grackle's mating call.

*

Observation #39: The policemen on horses do not deter the crowd. It is almost as if the policemen on horses are not welcome. ACAB, we shout in glee. ACAB. ACAB.

*

Observation #47: My friend Paul is so drunk I could steal his nose right off his face. I don't steal his nose, but I am reminded of our first kiss at the house party. The lights were loud and I could taste the music in my mouth. My molars hurt. His face has always been elegant.

*

Observation #90: I never prayed to be different but I did pray to forget. The forgetting begat a DUI. The DUI begat a court date. The court date begat second helpings of shame.

*

Observation #65: It is five hours until kickoff. I want to tell a joke about the last time I got off, but I can't remember the punchline.

American Airlines always pats me down extra.

*

Observation #17: The air can't decide if it's wet or ice-dry. It kisses up my calves like a snake, like a man. It knows what's waiting there. I won't charge it just to look.

*

Observation #3: The sky yellows. The crowd bellows. The game, like many things, is cancelled.

*

Observation #80: The policemen's horses let out swollen shits on the pavement. The police, generally speaking, are useless.

When did ghosts decide to keep silent?

*

Observation #72: I would rather be huddled in this shelter, counting the premature whiskers on Mark's face, than throwing up in a dive bar, but here I am doing both. Except this time it's not my vomit, it's everyone else's, and the shelter is the dive bar and heaven is hell and Rilke was right: every angel is terrifying.

My body is an angel and my friends' bodies are angels and every body that has ever come before our bodies is an angel, spreading feathered wings against AIDS and Prop 8 and Wyoming fence posts, swallowing broken teeth in the face of an elephant grave and wishing, always, for the game to stop.

THERE'S NOTHING QUITE LIKE TAKING A SHOT OF BOTTOM-SHELF WHISKEY

For Nellie

from the bottle, furtively, while your sister on the phone whispers from Ohio,
I'm putting down the cat. It's three in the morning where you are—which is where?
when did you last button your coat correctly on the first try?—
which is not Ohio, perhaps some other dry plain. Your sister details

the room: gray walls, fluorescent lights like thorns. Kind nurses sound strained.
Your sister purchases an expensive vase for ashes. *It's just a cat*, you want
to tell her. *Cats can't even talk.* Still, she is there & you are not. You are not anywhere.
Your cabinet opens again & again. Your rough hands crack open another bottle.

Your jeans unwashed for weeks. Your brother-in-law pays for the entire
mercy, sweet syringe & all. You won't pay him back. *She's quiet*, your sister breathes
into the phone. *Her paws have stopped running.* & what had she been after, anyway?
All those years spent asleep or sulking! As if she'd had nothing better to do.

It's the year of the cicadas, & she'll never get to smell their crisp
brown bodies or hold thin, brittle insect legs under her knife-like tongue.
Won't get to crunch their wings like bones. As a kitten, she would clamp her jaw
around the faucet & suck all day, nursing from a man-made metal breast.

Another update: *I think her heart is slowing.* You imagine racetracks,
but instead of horses, great big cats, eating-machines, door-scratchers, bulimic
house pets, your cat last in line. She's smaller than the other killers. White & orange
fur like autumn a hazy halo around her ribs. Hadn't you read somewhere that cat

piss is acidic? Your landlord—that slumlord!—says that's why you can't adopt,
but you think that's just an excuse. Maybe he just doesn't want you to be happy.
It's true, though: One cat can destroy a hardwood floor without a moment's thought.
You think about the walls you've ruined, the doorframes, an odd window or two.

Your hands were not born curled. You're out of alcohol & your sister is still talking. *I know*, you say. *I know*. & you don't know what exactly it is you know, but it seems to help, & there's nothing a small white lie can't fix. *Her eyes are closed*, she says. You don't need the transcript this time. What animal would look death in the eye?

Your cat's left iris, once bright green, had milked & clouded with age.
This has been a long time coming. How dare death still surprise you.
As if on autopilot, you cup the phone to your ear & say, *I love you*.
I love you. I love you. It's easier than being there.

MULBERRIES

a slew of mulberries
tiny suicides
so appealing on the sidewalk
and so unsure

WHEN WE'VE BEEN MARRIED NEARLY A YEAR, MY WIFE AND I SHARE A TOOTHBRUSH FOR THE FIRST TIME

Power out.
Tree resting on the telephone wire like a watchman.
Cannot see through bathroom window.
New addition to a new house.
Nothing to see through bathroom window.

*

Will food spoil in the freezer.
Will brain spoil in the silence.

*

No baby to comfort during storm.
No baby no time.
And God said to Rachel.
And God said to Mary.
He does not say to us.

*

And God said *Remi.*
God said *Remi if I'd wanted you to have children I'd have given you a penis.*

*

We are not His chosen grief-birds.
Lightning outside like a flashlight in my gray matter.
Hello, hello.
Is anyone there.

*

Unhelpful weatherman didn't predict this.
He is probably at home with his perfect family.
He is probably taking his penis for granted.

*

Darkness setting me up like a cruel trick.
I am worried that the sunlight will expire.

*

The silicone of my prosthetic penis absorbing sweat and ruin.
The silicone of my prosthetic penis reminding me.

*

How young we were when I said would you like to give me my injection.
How young we were when you took the syringe in your hand and coaxed it gently into my thigh.
How young we were when you licked the Testosterone from my leg, straightened your hair, and ran your perfectly crooked teeth over the needle-print.
How young we were when you lent me back, parted my knees, and said, listen, this is what I came for.

*

The kick in your belly is not a phantom because your belly has never housed anything.
The kick in your belly is desire.

*

The house creaking is a warning.
Even new carpentry can fail.

*

Time for bed but still no power.
Time for bed but why make love if it will leave us disappointed.
We must still care for our mouths.

*

I find one aggressively large Colgate toothbrush.
You find one hopelessly small tube of toothpaste.
Neither of us vocalizes what we are about to do.
Power might come back on later.
Who knows who will be there to see it.

WE'RE IN THE CAR ON MAIN STREET & IT'S DARK

1. outside. headlights glide past us like luminescent whales. the moon is out (or it's not). the car's name is Lorna (or it's not). a gift from my grandmother that I will eventually wreck.

2. inside. *Songs for Swingin' Lovers* stashed inside the glove compartment. beige seats overwhelm me. the steering wheel, fake leather, rough under my shaking hands. I grip it carefully between my knuckle-teeth so we don't crash because I am drunk.

3. underwater. each firefly outside the window perhaps, in actuality, a florescent jellyfish. your voice like the scream of pink or purple coral moments before they are un-reefed. a tree branch too close to the windshield.

4. in my head. small traumas like cereal overdosing beyond the box. and then: four-legged distraction too quick for .31 BAC. the two of us holding hands as if no one has ever held a hand before but it's not a hand, it's a mouse or a rat or a possum nesting in the sticky jugular dark & the windshield shatters into tiny pieces that want my jugular. & there are other cars & there is noise & there are many sea owls in my brain. the white darkness of the stars burns the rubber off the tires in an elegant, sea-star pattern while I remember what it was like to own a pet dog. the way a creature needed me but could tear out my arteries had it wanted to.

5. when I wake. you are not there & that is to be expected. I am still drunk. I dream this night over (& over), smooth the pillow next to me (& my body). the porch light turns itself on when I come without you. a lifetime of revision, of orange spots lighting up my liver.

MY BROTHER DIED

my brother died I tell the store clerk who drops the lemons, tiny suns bagged perfectly in expensive recycled paper, in shock not because of my brother's death but because of my violating the social script; *my brother died* I tell the JCPenney sales associate when she asks if I need a smaller size even though I'm clearly drowning in the sleeves so the question isn't so much a question as it is an indictment; *my brother died* I say on local television but only in my dreams because neither he nor I are (were) important enough to merit recognition; *my brother died* I type, failing to understand that my brother's death is not a question, into the glowing Google search bar reflected in my home office windows which are dark because it is nighttime and my friends are all asleep with un-dead brothers; *my brother died* I tell the telemarketer offering me a free cruise around the Bermuda Triangle and who without a beat tells me *that's okay sir we have a bereavement package have you ever kissed a volcano*; *my brother died* I tell my wife in bed before and after we attempt to make love but we can't because I keep getting distracted by how smooth my inner elbow is and how my brother's forearms had been tracked with pain; *my brother died* I tell my priest and he gasps, takes a step back, as if his very religion weren't based on the ugly death of a beautiful man; *my brother died* I want to scream at his dealer but I can't because the habit relies on secrecy and his dealer is therefore protected by anonymity; *my brother* died I tell the crosswalk signal when it tells me to *WAIT* but I cross the street anyway like an armadillo begging belly-up and if the sidewalk swallows me for jaywalking I'll just sink in and say *my brother died, my brother died, my brother died, and no one was there to stop it.*

REMI, IN THE NIGHT

Your voice split my eardrum this dark morning, sharp
gasp alighting stereocilia & cochlea a million
miles—which is to say one mile—away.

A strange cough has married itself to your lungs,
your heart like a vine. I wonder if smoking in our last
lifetime has blackened your insides to the point of no
return. Here there be monsters, maybe.

Has my loneliness eaten my brain? Chewed out
gray matter & replaced it with your croaked longing?
Remi so near I could feel it in my skull like a whale-

bellow. It's said that whales can talk. Not like
humans, but like whales. We are always talking.

I remember our first date when you were not
sick. I paid with a wallet I couldn't afford & you
pretended, *Remi, don't,* both of us dizzy in pleasure.
How were we to know the silence? I've never been
a Galileo.

But I see you, sometimes, in the sky. Your arms
like Orion. Elbow bent like a bow. Hand
pleading like a shield.

You are mythologized in every map except the oncologist's
prescription pad. I want to tear out your diagnosis
with my teeth, glinting gold from years of sloth. I have filled
my recklessness with expense. Tumors have filled yours with growth

spots burrowing into nerve & bone. (No, I don't know
how this works.) Where I, *Remi*, used to fill you. I fill a spare
mattress, instead, don't bother removing my dirty
socks. I brush my teeth before bed & wait for more
news. I wait for your voice in the night.

WHEN THE WORLD ENDED,

Golden shovel after Emily Dickinson

we couldn't find our passports. I
looked in the sandbox, in the shed—I heard
them crying out under the bed, maybe, like a
child sick from nightmares. One fly
sticking to the window. We remembered the buzz
of a Sunday hangover, spiraling nights with friends when
we could afford such luxuries. Now I
am sober and the bars have died.

Bombs sounded across the
globe, ethereal creatures breaking the stillness
of heat. We couldn't find our passports in
dusty attics or kitchen drawers or the
gas tank filled with fumes. Not in the lived-in room.

The recycling bin came up empty. The dog was
playing dead, as always, like
a corpse ballooned under a street lamp moon, the
mailman never sure what to say. The dog's stillness
the first warning sign we missed. What is the cataclysm in

this life? When does a marriage become the
cutting board of two strangers? The air
conditioning sang timidly between
our arguments and ultimatums. The
vows we'd exchanged caught under our tongues, heaving
resentment, maybe. My mouth of
diamonds. Your mouth of storm.

Acknowledgments

The following poems or variations thereof have appeared in these journals and anthologies:

"Are You Okay, Mike Flanagan?" (*The Rupture*, 2022)

"At a baseball game in ninety-degree weather, the man in front of me" (*West Trade Review*, 2023)

"Baptism | Before I Grew Up, There Was a War" (*Iron Horse Literary Magazine*, *Verse Daily*, 2023)

"Dead Name" (*Best New Poets*, 2021)

"Dear Hiring Committee:" (*Ice Queen Mag*, 2022)

"First" (*trampset*, 2022)

"Football Tailgate: Field Notes" (*Sport Literate*, 2022)

"from acorn to oak, or, after but not because of surviving the unsurvivable, i become a man" (*Diode*, 2023)

"Ghazal for the Bumps on My Spine" (*the minnesota review*, 2022)

"Gifts" (*Whale Road Review*, 2022)

"Gravedigger" (*new words {press}*, 2023)

"Linked Haiku with Ex-Boyfriend & Tree Sap" (*Call Me [Brackets]*, 2020)

"mulberries" (*Molecule Lit Mag*, 2022)

"my brother died" (*West Trade Review* Online Exclusive, 2023)

"Ninety Days" (*Chestnut Review*, 2022)

"On Learning of a Friend's Suicide While Waiting in Line at the Local Taco Bell" (*FreezeRay Poetry*, 2022)

"*Remi*, in the Night" (*The Missouri Review* Poem of the Week, 2023)

“Remi with Ghost & Joan of Arc” & “Paying for top surgery is like going to debtor’s prison” (*Cream City Review*, 2023)

“Sailor’s Knot” & “When the world ended,” (*Couplet Poetry*, 2022)

“Sinker” (*Divot Lit*, 2022)

“Tabernacle” (*Prairie Schooner*, 2022)

“The Lights” (*jmww,* 2022)

“The Men at Home” (*Poetry South*, 2022)

“There’s nothing quite like taking a shot of bottom-shelf whiskey” (*After Happy Hour Review*, 2022)

“Things I Can’t Tell My Landlord” (*Feral*, 2022)

“Triptych: To the People I Never Hit Drunk-Driving” (*Salamander*, 2022)

“We’re in the car on Main Street & it’s dark” (*Anti-Heroin Chic*, 2021)

“When We’ve Been Married Nearly a Year, My Wife and I Share a Toothbrush for the First Time” (*Bayou Magazine*, 2022)

“Your Therapist Has Surfer Dude Energy” (*Reunion: The Dallas Review*, 2024)

Notes

I am indebted to the good people at the Sundress Academy for the Arts Firefly Farms residency, where I wrote "Gifts" and conducted research on Mike Flanagan.

"When the world ended," is a golden shovel after Emily Dickinson's "I Heard a Fly Buzz When I Died" and was drafted at a Sundress Academy for the Arts CrossFit Workshop.

To learn more about Frank Dubois and other historical trans men, I recommend reading *True Sex: The Lives of Trans Men at the Turn of the Twentieth Century* by Emily Skidmore.

I would like to thank the *Orion* Environmental Writers' Workshop for giving me the space and time to write "The Men at Home" and "Things I Can't Tell My Landlord" with special thanks to Geffrey Davis for his invaluable mentorship and instruction there.

I would also like to thank the Palm Beach Poetry Festival and Matthew Olzmann for guidance in drafting "*Remi*, in the Night."

Thank you, also, to my Tulsa Glitterary Workshop cohort and Chen Chen for feedback on "We're in the car on Main Street & it's dark."

Thank you to Ken Hada and the Scissortail Creative Writing Festival for the opportunity to present some of these poems to an audience for the first time.

Thank you to Jacob Griffin Hall and Andy Bodinger for your insight on "from acorn to oak, or, after but not because of surviving the unsurvivable, i become a man" and for being the brilliant writers you are.

Thank you to my wonderful Ph.D. cohort at Oklahoma State University and MFA cohort at Bowling Green State University for shaping and challenging my poetic voice and inclinations.

Thank you to those who laid eyes on this book in its manuscript form and early stages, notably Sarah Beth Childers, Jonathan Coley, Whitney Koo, Lisa Lewis, Laura Minor, and, of course, my darling and forever first reader, Roseanna Recchia.

Thank you to Saint Andrew's Episcopal Church for forming me in body and soul and in whose pews many of these poems were drafted.

Thank you to my parents for moving us across the country with our infant daughter, fluffy boys, and a twenty-foot U-Haul truck for little-to-no recompense, and to Allyn Bernkopf and Sophie Roberts for loading the truck.

Lastly, thank you to my OG sobriety cats, Bean, Blossom, and Blueberry.

"How Will We Go on Living" is a cento. The source material is, in order of appearance, as follows:

1. "The Hole" by Ari Banias
2. "As a Human Being" by Jericho Brown
3. "Outing, Iowa" by Oliver Bendorf
4. "The Double Image" by Anne Sexton
5. "Lake Champlain at Flood Level" by Eli Clare
6. "Barbie Chang's Tears" by Victoria Chang
7. "Martsa's" by Kit Yan
8. "/bower to bower/" by Nico Peck
9. "The Law" by Gerald Stern
10. "A Prayer After All" by John Berryman
11. "Fourth-Grade Soundtrack" by Mary Ardery
12. "Henry by Night" by John Berryman
13. "The Parking Lot" by Max Wolf Valerio
14. "The Sacrifice" by Frank Bidart
15. "Confessional" by Frank Bidart
16. "They went to sea in a sieve" from "The Jumblies" by Edward Lear
17. "Dreams" by Nikki Giovanni
18. "San Antonio" by Naomi Shihab Nye

19. *The Lumberjack's Dove*, Part IV, by Gennarose Nethercott
20. "Delirium, II: Alchemy of the Word" by Arthur Rimbaud, trans. Louise Varese
21. "Geomancy" by F. Daniel Rzicznek
22. "Although clumsy" by Sappho
23. "Written in the church-yard at Middleton in Sussex" by Charlotte Smith
24. *The Book of Frank*, Part I, by CA Conrad
25. "101.133.422" by Josh Bettinger
26. "Behind Yellow Tape" by Reginald Dwayne Betts
27. "E Tenebris" by Oscar Wilde
28. "The Wilde Woman of Aiken" by Robin Coste Lewis
29. "A Requiem for the Homeless Spirits" by Timothy Liu
30. "When I Realize I'm Wearing My Girlfriend's Ex-Girlfriend's Panties" by Angel Nafis
31. "Chinese Umbrella" by Ralph Angel
32. "Night" by William Blake
33. "Moon" from *The Oxford Dictionary of Nursery Rhymes*, eds. Iona & Peter Opie
34. "On the Road to Sri Bhuvaneshwari, Part IV," by Robin Coste Lewis
35. "Texture" by Gwendolyn Zepeda
36. "What Work Is" by Philip Levine
37. "The Lord Might Have Given Him Wings" by Reginald Dwayne Betts
38. "Dovetailed" by Roseanna Alice Boswell
39. "ABC Haibun" by Helli Fang
40. "In Search of Evanescence, Part 3," by Agha Shahid Ali
41. "Ghazal of an Island" by John Drury
42. "Feast or Famine" by Tarfia Faizullah
43. "Exchanging Vows, Part IV: Advice for Newlyweds" by Janine Joseph
44. "Fire Water" by Tyree Daye
45. "As if my lips have learned to weep" by Simon Perchik
46. "Dream Animal" by Yusef Komunyakaa
47. "XI. Interrogation Chamber" by Aria Aber

48. “A House in Nicosia” by Jennifer Kwon Dobbs
49. “Beetle” by Jennifer Kwon Dobbs
50. “The Whetting of Teeth” by Jamaal May
51. “to the mulberry tree” by Ross Gay
52. “Dreaming of Hair” by Li-Young Lee
53. “at the down-low house party” by Danez Smith
54. “The Verging Cities” by Natalie Scenters-Zapico
55. #9 from “Poems of the Imagination” by William Wordsworth
56. “summer, somewhere” by Danez Smith
57. “SOS” by Amiri Baraka
58. The City in Which I Love You” by Li-Young Lee
59. “An Empty House Is a Debt” by Diana Khoi Nguyen
60. “Landscape with Fruit Rot and Millipede” by Richard Siken
61. “Advent” by Claire Wahmanholm
62. “the opening” by Ross Gay
63. “Ladybirds” by Larissa Szporluk
64. “Fall Parties” by Becca Klaver
65. “How to Be Perfect” by Ron Padgett
66. “In the Baggage Room at Greyhound” by Allen Ginsberg
67. “Pine Cones” by Naomi Shihab Nye
68. “My 1986” by Stephanie Burt
69. “The giver [for Berdis]” by James Baldwin
70. “How to Be Perfect” by Ron Padgett
71. “Wolf OR-7” by Natalie Diaz
72. “Night a ladder we climb to reach” by Ely Shipley
73. “Landscape with one of the earthworm’s ten hearts” by Laura Kasischke
74. “How Can I Give Fewer Fucks” by Taisia Kitaiskaia
75. “The Unseen Hand of Zombie Jesus” by Jamaal May
76. “Tobacco Origin Story” by Joy Harjo
77. “The First Elegy” by Rilke
78. “Operation Cyclone, Years Later” by Aria Aber
79. ”I’m Nobody! Who are you?” by Emily Dickinson

80. “Holding You Sober Close to Me” by Ralph Angel
81. “This Room and Everything in It” by Li-Young Lee
82. “American Sonnet 95” by Wanda Coleman
83. “The Secretary Chant” by Marge Piercy
84. “Blossom” by Dorianne Laux
85. “Red All Over” by Robin Coste Lewis
86. “Prayer to my lady of Paphos” by Sappho
87. “Above the World” by Philip Levine
88. “Wetback” by Marcelo Hernandez Castillo
89. “Portrait in Seafoam and Offshore Lights” by C. Dale Young
90. “Tales of a Lost Boyhood, Part 9: The Bicycle Parade” by Samuel Ace
91. “Ode to the Beloved’s Hips” by Natalie Diaz
92. “The Double Image” by Anne Sexton
93. “Lady Lazarus” by Sylvia Plath
94. “Patron” by Oliver Bendorf
95. “Coolie” by Rajiv Mohabir
96. “Canticle 6” by May Sarton
97. “When the Dead Ask My Father About Me” by Sharon Olds
98. “The Great Fires” by Jack Gilbert
99. “The Sleepers” by Walt Whitman
100. “Nights and Days” by Adrienne Rich

About the Author

Remi Recchia is a Lambda Special Prize-winning poet, essayist, and editor from Kalamazoo, Michigan. An eight-time Pushcart Prize nominee, his work has appeared in *World Literature Today*, *Best New Poets 2021*, and *Best of the Net 2025*, among others. He is the author of two collections of poetry and four poetry chapbooks, and he is the editor of two contemporary poetry anthologies. Remi has received support from institutions such as Tin House, PEN America, and the Poetry Foundation. He holds an MFA in poetry and a Ph.D. in English. Remi is currently pursuing an M.Div. at Yale University. He lives in Connecticut with his wife, daughter, and two cats.

21st Century Poets

21st Century Poets is a collection of full-length poetry books by TRP authors whose first book of poetry was released after the year 2000.

BOOKS IN THIS SERIES:

No. 001 — Kendall Dunkelberg — *Time Capsules*
No. 002 — William Bedford Clark — *Blue Norther and Other Poems*
No. 003 — Karla K. Morton — *Names We've Never Known*
No. 004 — Ben Greer — *The Bright House*
No. 005 — Beryl Lawn — *Poems from Both Sides of the Fence*
No. 006 — Swep Lovitt — *Sometimes the World Is Too Beautiful*
No. 007 — William Wright — *Bledsoe*
No. 008 — Sarah Cortez — *Walking Home*
No. 009 — Jesse Graves — *Tennessee Landscape with Blighted Pine*
No. 010 — Richard Boada — *The Error of Nostalgia*
No. 011 — Sarah Cortez — *Cold Blue Steel*
No. 012 — David Havird — *Map Home*
No. 013 — Beryl Lawn — *More Poems from Both Sides of the Fence*
No. 014 — Jesse Graves — *Basin Ghosts*
No. 015 — Karla K. Morton — *A Constant State of Leaping*
No. 016 — Kendall Dunkelberg — *Barrier Island Suite*
No. 017 — Stephen Gibson — *The Garden of Earthly Delights*
No. 018 — Karla K. Morton — *Accidental Origami: New and Selected Works*
No. 019 — Karla K. Morton — *Wooden Lions*
No. 020 — Mary Morris — *Enter Water, Swimmer*
No. 021 — Elisabeth Murawski — *Heiress*
No. 022 — Randall Watson — *The Geometry of Wishes*

No. 023 — Sarah Kain Gutowski — *Fabulous Beast*

No. 024 — Jennifer Sperry Steinorth — *A Wake with Nine Shades*

No. 025 — Mary Morris — *Dear October*

No. 026 — Andrew Hemmert — *Sawgrass Sky*

No. 027 — Matt W. Miller — *Tender the River*

No. 028 — Jesse Graves — *Tennessee Landscape with Blighted Pine* (10th Anniversary Edition)

No. 029 — Forrest Rapier — *As the Den Burns*

No. 030 — Sarah Audsley — *Landlock X*

No. 031 — Luke Johnson — *Quiver*

No. 032 — Sarah Kain Gutowski — *The Familiar*

No. 033 — Joshua Robbins — *Eschatology in Crayon Wax*

No. 034 — Theodora Ziolkowski — *Ghostlit*

No. 035 — Kimberly Ann Priest — *tether & lung*

No. 036 — Mary Morris — *Lanterns in the Night Market*

No. 037 — Daniel Lassell — *Frame Inside a Frame*

No. 038 — Luke Johnson — *Distributary*

No. 039 — Brooke Sahni — *In This Distance*

No. 040 — Randall James Tyrone — *City of Dis*

No. 041 — Ryan Vine — *The Cave*

No. 042 — Aaron Baker — *American Experiment*

No. 043 — Lauren Camp — *Is Is Enough*

No. 044 — Donovan McAbee — *Holy the Body*

No. 045 — Alex Mouw — *The Unbelieving Yelp of Prey*

No. 046 — Remi Recchia — *Addiction Apocalypse*